The Last Coherent Thing

The Last Coherent Thing

Poems by

John Wing Jr.

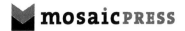 mosaicPRESS

Library and Archives Canada Cataloguing in Publication

Title: The last coherent thing / John Wing.

Names: Wing, John, Jr., 1959- author.

Description: Poems.

Identifiers: Canadiana (print) 20210169753
            Canadiana (ebook) 20210169796

ISBN 9781771615686 (softcover) ISBN 9781771615693 (PDF)
ISBN 9781771615709 (EPUB) ISBN 9781771615716 (Kindle)

Classification: LCC PS8595.I5953 L37 2021
                DDC C811/.54—dc23

Published by Mosaic Press, Oakville, Ontario, Canada, 2021.

MOSAIC PRESS, Publishers
www.Mosaic-Press.com
Copyright © John Wing 2021

Cover design by Rahim Piracha

Printed and bound in Canada

ONTARIO ARTS COUNCIL
CONSEIL DES ARTS DE L'ONTARIO
an Ontario government agency
un organisme du gouvernement de l'Ontario

Funded by the Government of Canada
Financé par le gouvernement du Canada

Canada

ONTARIO CREATES

Mosaic Press
1252 Speers Road, Units 1 & 2, Oakville, Ontario, L6L 5N9
(905) 825-2130 • info@mosaic-press.com • www.mosaic-press.com

For John Malcolm Wing, 1930 – 2017

Table of Contents

AUTO-BIOPSY

A Broken Fever

The river is audible in my dreams.
It gurgles, wordless.

The highway calls. The hard-rubber
scream of motion, of leaving.

My mouth opens, but the throat constricts
because I'm always late, running.

And I realize that this discovery
isn't in the realm of Wallace in Ternate,

waking from a broken fever and writing
out the theory of natural selection in one go.

No, just something noticed again
after noticing it thousands of other times

under the bank of the audible river.
Under the moss.

When I Was A Boy

This is how old I am:
When I was a boy, parents vaccinated their children
without a thought.
Mother would bring me in, *"How many does he need?*
Eight? Ok. Let's go. Stick him. Stick him again.
Stop crying you little bastard. Do the one in the butt.
The polio one. I've been threatening him with that."

I have a vivid memory of being examined
by a pediatrician for an hour in his office at age six.
And he smoked for the whole exam. At the end
he said, *"You seem pretty healthy, kid. A touch*
of asthma. You'll probably grow out of that."

Parents would often do things - try
not to get angry here - without consulting us.
There were no family conferences in which
we had what might loosely be termed a vote.

This is how old I am:
We would get up in the morning,
run downstairs, open the back door,
and there, on the back steps: Milk. Free milk.
Bottle of milk, bottle of cream, bottle of Beep.
Who remembers Beep?
It was an orange drink made out of chickens.

The guy who brought
the milk came in a wagon pulled by a horse.
The dairy, Silverwoods, had a stable.

And all the milk bottles smelled vaguely
of horseshit.

When I was a boy,
Tim Horton was a *guy*.
With a crewcut.
On the television.
Which had thirteen channels,
(nine of them were CBC).

There was one TV in the house.
My parents called it *The Idiot Box*.
No we have the Idiot Phone, but
Idiot is a long word, so we just call it
The I-phone.

Back then the word for 'cool' was, "cool".
Now it's 'dank'. My wife and I were in line at the movies.
Two teenaged girls in front of us didn't realize
we could hear them.
I think they thought they were texting.

One said, "*How was the sex?*" And the other replied,
"*Oh my God, it was dank. SO dank. Really dank.*"
And I said, "*It was damp and it smelled bad, really?*
You know you should shower first, right?"

When I was a boy, if a man and woman
were going to meet up for sex, it was called
an *assignation*, a *tryst*. A one-night stand,
or, in my case, an Act Of God. Nowadays,
it's called a Hook-up, meaning what?

You tow the girl over to where you fuck her?
Pretty soon it'll be an app. The iPoke.
Or, if you can't find a partner, the selfie.
"*I'm going to stay home tonight. Rub out a selfie.
I've got a new selfie-stick I want to try out.*"

When I was a boy, if I wanted to learn something,
I had to go to the library, stand in line, get a pass
for the reference room, go there, get one of those
wrist-spraining encyclopedias, open it to my topic,
read the entry, read it again, make notes, and copies
at ten cents a throw. And if I couldn't spell
what I wanted to look up, it went unlearn-ed.

Which is why I'm a comedian today,
and not a Psychiatrist.

Spelling isn't necessary now.
I typed TOTE BAGS into Google the other day
and it came back, *Did you mean
big tits, John?* Google knows me.

This is how old I am:
The last time the Maple Leafs
won the Stanley Cup,
I was alive.

Medical Agenda

This is going to hurt, the nurse says,
steadying the back of my hand
for the needle. She smiles
as it goes in. Knowing it will
hurt makes it easier.
You know you're getting anaesthesia
for this procedure? Yes, I know.
Do you know what kind?
What kind? No.
You're getting propyphol. You
know what that is? It's the drug
that killed Michael Jackson.
The doctor stops by before I lose
consciousness. *There's a one-in-four-thousand*
chance of a perforation of your colon, he says.
How many have you done today? I ask.
He laughs, but he's gone.
Far away already.
I awake from a Kafka story, *In the Renal Colony*.
The doctor swims into my eyeline,
holding photos of a dark canal.
All good, he says.
Diagnoses come by e-mail,
good news
or phone call, *bad*.

Houdini

I spent the night in an emergency ward.
This was long ago, when I still believed death
was far away, like summer seems in February.

I was weak and covered with lesions. A doctor examined me
and then left, saying a room would be available in the morning.
I lay on my back, noting the traffic from the main entrance
to the right,
and the door with the combination number-lock on the left.

Doctors, striding the way people with those kinds
of bank accounts stride, went through the number-lock door,
and I stayed awake long enough to know the correct sound
that opened it.

There was a room across the hall, where they brought an
older man,
undressed him, and placed him in a bed I couldn't see.
He was limping. A doctor and a nurse spoke to him and then
left.
Then he got up, dressed, and shuffled toward the main door
on the right.

A few minutes later, two nurses brought him back, undressed,
gowned, and bedded him again. One nurse lectured him in a
kindly-stern way. Then they both left.

Five minutes later, I saw him dress himself again,
and after some is-the-coast-clear looks he headed for the
main door

a second time. He almost made it, too. It was a half hour
before they frog-marched him back, but it felt much longer.
I suppose time passes slowly when you don't know you're
    going to die,
And quickly if you do.

The third time he was spoken to harshly by a doctor and a
    nurse,
and he stayed in bed a while, but then I noticed him dressing
    again,
and then standing at his door, peeking out.

A doctor flashed past, the number lock engaged on the door,
and as soon as it did, he went zipping out the secure way.
Gone, not to return.

That long night, and days after, no one could figure out
what was wrong with me. Once they did, it took months
to fully recover. Much of it blurs, yet I remember
the old Houdini, slipping his shackles, refusing
to die where they told him.

Recovering Addict

Your disease never stops whispering in your ear.
Needling you. Suggesting
you could so totally handle it now.
What could it hurt?
Who's gonna know?
No matter how far you get from
your last drink, your last buzz;
no matter how confident you get about the distance,
or how many years you add up in single days,
your disease does not sleep.
It watches you sleep,
thinking, he'll be awake soon,
we'll talk then.

The Red Suitcase

Sobriety is so much to unpack.
The addict years are ones you don't get back

There are stickers on the faded red vinyl,
reminding me of places I traveled
but have no memories that mark them.
The inside still smells of smoke.
I've been sober years longer
(eight, as of this writing) than I was high,
drunk, or a combination of the two,
but it doesn't change the partially unpacked
bag in the closet, not as heavy as it once was,
perhaps, yet still full.

A pile of undealt cards awaited me that first year.
Pain bubbling up from nowhere, anger wells so deep
you couldn't hear the bucket splash. All new, packed
beautifully in my red suitcase. Each exposed in real time,
in real place, in unmedicated agony. I saw everything
I hadn't wished to see, felt everything I'd chosen
not to feel, and kept returning to the bag, figuring
it would be, if not empty, then lighter each time,
easier to carry around. But it wasn't. I still take
a deep breath before I lift it.

The lies come so easily at first.
I can handle it – I don't need it. It's easy
to forget missing work all those days
because of 'allergies'. But the first painlessness;
the feeling that this is who I am when no one hates me

or critiques me or wishes failure on me, this isn't
the fake-person-face I paint on to please, it's just
me in my tiny apartment where the bed comes out
of the sofa and the room disappears, *that* feeling
grows and will never go away.

At 23, I spent a crucial year on unemployment,
free afternoons in a friend's basement pad,
getting high. I was laughing hysterically at nothing
there the day John Belushi died. *That won't happen to me,*
I thought, if I thought about it at all.
I began to make money by the end of that year,
so I could start buying my own drugs, which led to
getting high alone. For addicts, it really helps
to like the solitude. You wind up preferring it.
Your own voices, your own traveling company.

The addict-years pile up, so don't look back
Sobriety is so much to unpack

I didn't recognize when it stopped being a hobby.
But it was the moment I began making rules.
Never get high less than two hours before a show.
Don't spark up before noon on those rare days
I actually woke up before noon.
Never carry at an airport, or through customs.
Fresh shirts – breath mints. *Never audition high –*
even if the role is a stoner. How to carry,
how not to carry. I ceased living my life
and begin living strategies of concealment.

Concealment is so simple, as it turns out.
The world sees your stoned face and doesn't realize

there's a sober one. So the farce is played by all
for a while. No one can get close enough
to see all your faces, but that's a good thing.
Occasionally you interlude with another addict,
but that gets old quickly. You recognize the faces
of others like an owl spotting a fat mouse in a meadow.
You live your addiction like a marriage,
forsaking all others.

I couldn't score in Winnipeg one week.
Took four agonizing days to find a quarter-ounce,
then had ten days to smoke all of it, because
I had to fly back to L.A. Strained it and rolled
thirty-two joints. Broke my no-more-than-two-a-day
rule in order to finish it. I couldn't let it go to waste.
Had an intense nap-dream one afternoon. I was on
my deathbed, apologizing for everything between sobs.
I awoke and wondered if such a destiny
could be changed. I flew home and tried to stop.

The first years of not using brought up all the pain,
resentment, anger, and father-issue-Catholic shit
I'd been desperately holding down with drugs .
The red suitcase bulged at the seams. Every time
I opened it I wasn't sure I could get it shut again.
I finally began to mature from adolescent to adult, which
was a good thing, since I was thirty-five years old
and already a parent. I found AA, and find it still.
I'm John, and I'm an alcoholic-addict.
Hi, John. Today I was remembering…

Sobriety is so much to unpack
So we remember everything in black.

In a car once, I smoked half a joint,
then put the remainder in my shoe,
in case we were stopped by the cops.
Two hours later, wanting to get high again,
I went looking for it and couldn't remember
where it was. The search got a little desperate
and at one point I began to cry. My new wife,
who was driving, watched me in a peculiar state
of pity-shock. I was twenty-nine years old, and still
had six years left that will never be retrieved.

Grapevine

Word comes down,
a rolling-rock telegram.
He's drinking again.

Got sober a few years
back, when a marriage ended
and a hip was replaced.

Last year's visit, smiled
when he said, *As it turns out
not an alcoholic.*

*Can have one if I want
and not worry about it.*
Hoped my nod didn't give

away the struggle not to tell
my five-decades friend how
full of shit he was.

Now, he has one
when he wants,
which is often.

Our disease is the only one
where the sure belief you don't have it
is a symptom.

For me, it comes effortlessly
from the Irish mother of my
Irish grandmother.

A log-line of mean drunks,
potheads, vein-shooters,
and broken-glass anger.

Add my decades to a century
of bad behavior
in a disease disguise.

The longer I'm sober,
the less it seems like
an accomplishment.

Stunted, never to act
my age, never to catch
up to confidence.

In atonement's
drudgery, remembering
the deliciousness.

Dying to say something
to my dying friend, something
he won't like at all.

At the same time,
jealous of his journey
back down the slide.

The Real Power

This new search, and it could be the last,
is for forgiveness. Not to seek others
and detect *OK* in their faces, the gentle
nostril-flare, the harvested forehead.
Forgiveness *in* me, not *for* me.

To find it, and let it out of the cave.
Cure the memory-pus tumors.
Forgive the choices, the lies, the swag
sold for a song, the piled debts, the vault *IOUs*,
my crimes.

A caregivers' conceit-concert.
Brief reflections of might-have
and long ago possibility.
A narcissist drinking deeply
from a mirror.

This has become my search, through
the webbed attic crawlspaces,
the glimmered addiction-years,
trying to find the real power
to stop eating poison.

Biopsy Driving

One must never be late for bad news.
Driving to an early appointment,

The CT scan showed something, I'm afraid.

I leave two hours ahead, figuring forty minutes
in normal traffic, though morning in L.A. is never normal

Second biopsy for this little problem,

I make some early, on-the-fly route changes,
turning right where I would normally go left,

charmingly called a 'mass' by one doctor,
and a 'thing' by another.

taking this street to avoid a stretch of freeway
which will undoubtedly be backed up.
I've lived here thirty years, so I know
a hundred routes to everywhere.

A benign thing or a malignant thing?
We don't know.

Turning right was smart, and I congratulate myself,
finding the freeway four miles ahead, past
the choked-up section of grey hills that burned last fall.

The first result was inconclusive.
Wait three months, let it heal and we'll do it again.

The second freeway is crowded but not impassable.
I make a gut decision to get off at our old exit, Verdugo.
This was the first neighborhood I got to know
after moving here. It all comes back,
a left, a right, another right...

Come and we'll stick a big needle in your neck.

I pass our old street, our old apartment building.
We lived in three different apartments in six years here.
Looping around, I pass another freeway I will avoid,
take a right on Glendale Boulevard, and bear left to Rowena
to a left at Hyperion, all fairly clear.

What if it's malignant?
We take out your thyroid.
I don't need it?

In those years, this was my ambitious route
to the Hollywood comedy clubs.
Hyperion to Fountain, which, back then,
was the best east/west street, speed-wise.

Please download and sign these consent forms
and bring them with you.

I used to get my hair cut down here.
The barber advised me on how to impress
the Immigration people who would adjudicate
my green card application.
"Bring your wedding album," he said.
And we did. The salon, called Hair Dooz,
is long gone. A hardware store now.
The once and future Burrito King is a Pinkberry.

I've now been officially frightened for five months.

The only surviving landmark is Bogie's Liquor.
On our anniversary one year I hired a limo
to take us to a Hollywood restaurant, and on
the way home we had him stop in front of Bogie's
while I ran in and got ice cream.

This day hasn't been out of my thoughts.

That was when I could still surprise her.
Recalling it almost brings a tear and then
I slam on the brakes to avoid rear-ending someone.

Now it's here, answers approaching.

Traffic is good. I was smart to come this way.
I pass through Glassell Park, Silver Lake, Franklin Hills
and finally into Little Armenia, waiting for the interminable
       light
at Sunset, Virgil, Hillhurst and Hollywood,
a convergence of four streets going madly off in all directions.

I will die of something
and it might be this.

I turn left onto Sunset. Early, as always.
But I brought a book.
All contingencies have been considered

Except one.

Hiker-Gatherer

I want to go back and tell early man,
I hike now.

Along mountain trails in special flex-fiber shoes,
and thick sport-socks, greased in sunblock,
food and water safely slung behind,
measuring trails and climbs against my youthful best.

I don't go hungry when a hunt fails,
carry fire in a horn, or make my own clothes.
There are stores for that.

I take photos from high points,
stomp through bushes like a dominant predator,
watching carefully to avoid horseshit on the trail
as he once eluded snakes, wolves, death.

Would he recognize me if I could go back?
Trade his snow-leopard coat for my Gore-Tex windbreaker?
Share his meal with a fellow traveler?

A meal I'd gladly eat, being on the Paleo diet.
We could astound each other with home-made arrows
and Isotoner gloves. He'd laugh at what I couldn't smell.

A hundred thousand years ago,
water tore through this valley,
this dry wash where I hike.
A deep river the desert's forgotten.

But he survived here, aware of every odor, every sound.
Unaware of measured time, or perpetual motion theory.
Warmed by fire, dancing on cave walls, a light sleeper.

Today, in layered Lycra , bitching up the trail,
my shoes dusty with ancestor- bones,
I think of him, my long ago human relative.
His daily struggle, the hours passing slowly
between hunger, courage, and fear.

My silly envy for a simpler existence carried me
to the end of my healthy walk.
I should go back in time.
I've been putting that off.

Sneaking Towards Curtain

On the really fine days,
morning sex without knee pain,
perfect nostalgia coffee,
golf, perhaps tennis,
and shots to savour like a good steak,
and later a good steak, seared pink-maroon
something written,
nothing forgotten or left on.
Even on those days,
there are evening aches
to remind us of morning long gone.
The encroaching realization,
hiding in the pleasure
that the fine days are,
at best, finite.

GONE GIRL

Outbuildings

Once I was the house, the structure,
gabled and reaching upward, striving
like the trees I came from, good European
stock, a bone-soup boiled down through
centuries of swaddled culture.

I grew until the house couldn't hold me anymore,
the town abandoned like an unwanted child.
But it followed me, kept me company, the strength
of its steps, the attic isolation, the basement
full of sports dreams.

Everything I learned within its walls;
every light switch found with blind confidence,
every slightly raised nail on a high stair, or
shadow of a bat flying across a room again
and again. I left and carried every timber.

For many years afterward, as my search
intensified, I lived in rooms. One room, two
rooms, walkups, rooms without brothers
or sisters or even parents to judge
cleanliness, morality, addiction.

But in photos of me from that time, you
can see the house within, the sloping roof
of ambition, the determined driveway shoveled
clean after a blizzard, the hedges budding lime-green
when spring arrived to herald new games.

I lived in five places in eight years, or eight places
in fourteen years, between a move from my adopted
city to one where I would be lost. An outbuilding
on a farm where the aged owners rent the fields
to young strivers, shouldering houses.

As I traveled, always forgetting that I would
one day be old, I found cover in the brown house
built in 1912, in the stone basement where boys
played hockey, in the attic penthouse I called
my bedroom for twelve sponge-years.

And as I acquired knowledge of the road-packed
metropolis I made my final destination, I fastened
it to the grid structure of my original house-pedia,
where it would grow until I stopped. And somewhere
along its way another house was found.

Now I have lived longer in this place, this house
than anywhere. Longer in this town than anywhere.
A flat-roofed, no-basement bungalow in the Spanish style,
with a yard large enough to host many children's parties
and bury two dogs. Each year we fix something.

Built in 1924, survivor of earthquakes and other
plagues, the house my daughters took with them
when they left. And it will guide them through
the search years, the crawlspace-journeys,
the outbuildings.

To the Airport

We hug at curbside and she goes in,
swept into the current, the river of skin-traffic.
On the drive home, her mother remarks
that she left without looking back. And I think
that's probably not a bad thing,
though I don't say it out loud.

We're both on a sad edge.
This is the first time she's leaving
without any idea when she'll return.
Worries will increase, information scarce.
She's begun the next phase and we,
her inventors, aren't part of it anymore.

Just voices on the phone now.
E-mailers. Face-timers. Skype-types.
Part of a past life. On the drive back
to our now childless house,
I think that this is as it should be,
which I also don't say out loud.

Gone Girl

The dismantling of a child's room is necessary. thing
She's gone now. She lives the full land mass away,
another seaboard. Lives with the boyfriend-fiance.
They have jobs.

So I take apart the goddamn huge IKEA closet
she insisted on buying, box up the remaining clothes,
carry them out to the garage, full of the things
we bought her, piles of hope attracting a particular
kind of reproachful dust.

The room reveals secrets.
Things she cloaked in smiles
and an expectation of privacy.
Her drug stash, found with some bemusement.
Enough marijuana in the prescription vial for a single hit,
	perhaps?

A box of love letters from a boy I never knew fancied her.
A painting he did for her, painfully derivative, talentless,
A Qu'ran. He was a Muslim and wanted her to convert.
He didn't realize what he was dealing with, obedience-wise.

Soon the floor men will come, tear up the horrorshow
carpet, put down some plastic boards that look like wood.
I'll get bookcases, and her room will become an office-gues-
	troom.
We'll paint it a soothing colour; something that inspires me
to write poems about this child, who, fate willing, won't be
	back.

Wildlife

Having reached the age where every
phone call from a recognized number
begins with panic preparation,
I always start with 'Everything ok?'
Knowing her first word
will be evidence enough.

Sometimes the call
is so silly, so insignificant,
that I'm almost angry for feeling relieved.
But I never say "You called me
from three thousand miles away
to tell me there's a raccoon in your backyard?"

I laugh instead, and remember she calls
because she loves me, remember
she watched me call my father
every day for the first twenty years
of her life, so it's natural to seek me out
whenever wildlife appears.

Until I had a child,
I never knew real fear.

The Backward Glance

And so I didn't marry you
but someone else; and so the years
came down the way we didn't think
they would , predictions not quite true
or even close. Late stages clear
the backward glance, one naked blink

Explains the great mystery now,
aging parent and foolish child
shrink-wrapped into one, late for school.
And so the cities, journeys, tao
of expectation all redialed
to fit new paradigms, to duel

In new arenas. Lessons taught,
informed, infused, and in the slow
forgetful dance we found a trust
elsewhere, a love and knowledge bought
in rewrite and recall. And so
we didn't marry. Lucky us.

The Drift

A two-girlfriend day in a two-horse town
where none of us grew up.

The first, a college fling when I was forty years ago.
She's a lawyer, runs a clinic, talks of opioid addiction
and the threat of bad choices, while we noodle
over lattes in a trendy corner of this boring rainy town.

We play catch-up – this child, that husband, ailments
and anniversaries, such a long journey from our
little— met, dated, coupled, fought, recoupled, parted—trip.
Once we were young and lucky, now just lucky.

And we meet on this day for no real reason, other
than to note our luck, our occasional satisfactions,
and then return to the lives we made apart, spoken
about today because my drift passed through here.

She walks me to my car, and we hug under an umbrella,
shoulders touching briefly, the rest of us at ninety degrees.
"I'm still raw over how I treated you in college," I say.
And she laughs. The drift takes us back and forward and
    gone.

The second, a high school unrequited, a long Irish flame
encountered at music lessons and schools and recitals,
who I stared at often but never dared ask. Or if I did,
the drift has taken it and her response too far to see.

A teacher, now retired, married late and well, we lunch
at her home on ten acres, all large rooms and view.
And she talks of the boy she loved but couldn't get who
is my oldest friend, divorced, living forty minutes away.

Their drift was bent to find again. "But I heard he was gay,"
she says, which is odd because I never heard that, and he's
    not.
And the other boy she dated for a late high school year, my
best friend, whose drift took him far, almost all the way
    around.

I take out my phone and show her a photo of him
on the Thames two years ago. She looks and doesn't know
who it is. I show another photo of the one she loved, also
    from
two years past and she doesn't recognize him, either.

A two-girlfriend day in a two-horse town, where none
of us grew up. Some we got but didn't want. Some we loved
but couldn't tell. Some will never age or know a pale regret.

REM

Last night – for no reason,
you were in my dream.

We were at your house, watching
a ballgame, sitting on your red sofa.

Your husband sat between us.
He'd stopped dyeing his hair,

and finally looked as someone
his age should. I mentioned it.

He laughed. We talked some baseball
and some hockey. I couldn't get over

how good his hair looked. Then I saw
your hand , dangling across his shoulder-

blade, and it reached out and grasped
my bicep for a moment, squeezing,

to remind me that I was
dreaming of you.

Misplaced

What do I miss about you, years
removed from being sure
while it occurred around me,
but spent the lifetime after
questioning? I miss
everything you did.

Love on the hard boil,
touched first like an iron,
fingers hissing in wonder...
will this burn me? Will she
like this? Will this work?
Should I tell? Can I?

Young enough not to be
cemented in habit, OCD came
in middle age, or as I call it,
aged middle. Even liked my story.
Told it happily and with curiosity
for the unimagined turns.

Now every visible footstep
on the way back shows detours
rejected, paths with maybes
written all over them, now
might have beens. Nostalgia
for the unchosen.

And you, waking in passion,
flesh and idea springing to life.

Moments so perfect that the return
is regretless, the pleasure still sweet
like the ice cream we bought
from the boy who died.

I miss the way
you laughed when I was stupid,
which was so gentle and welcoming
that I stopped being afraid
of myself for two whole years
– imagine.

I don't miss the sex.
I miss being unmasked, unlost,
confident and in exactly the place
carved for me by time, living
momently, knowing everything
I needed to remember.

Now everything about me
in the decades since crowds in,
obscuring our time. The right reasons
were there and still are. Nothing harbored.
Memories are costumes, and I recall
how they felt first, on new skin.

We are Stardust

At 17, she went to Woodstock, somehow
securing permission. *I was there,* she would,
casually drop, like a handkerchief
she hoped you would retrieve.
She was beautiful the way hope is beautiful,
her hair the colour of dried blood.

I read accounts of the bacchanal at Yasgur's farm.
I watched the documentary, searching for her
face in every shot. She wore the same pair of jeans
the whole four days. Not that I didn't believe her.
I just wanted to find her youth in the history
of that muddy jamboree.

12 years later, she was an exotic redhead, managing
bands and a young impressionist, Jim Carrey, unknown then.
Her big act was Shox Johnson and the Jive Bombers,
unknown now. She was always around the comedy club that
was my university, looking for talent. We started talking one
    night
and went where conversation leads.

That spring, we simmered, thickening a friendship.
Coffee dates, new ideas, life stories. She was
7 years older, happily curious about almost everything,
and honest in a way that in later years made me wonder
why she chose show business. I was young enough
to think everything would be easy.

I once asked if she'd had sex at Woodstock, and she aimed
a look at me. *Silly* question. It was as though she'd gone
to the moon with 500,000 friends. In those four days,
it had birth and rebirth and afterbirth, growth and shape
and in air and time, and all with music playing. Her history
was history. She was Neil Armstrong, hanging out with me.

That summer, she decided to throw a party. She called it
The White Party. Everyone would wear white. A stolen kiss,
     surprisingly
passionate; an act of courageous timing I would never repro-
     duce
secured me an invitation. She took me shopping for some-
     thing white
and said when the party ended we would make love, making
     it
the only party I would ever attend with that assurance.

Many came; everyone gleaming in virgin-white, with my new
girlfriend resplendent in a maroon fringed toga-gown.
Liquor flowed, smoke plumed, hash, pot, laughter. It was
a microcosmic anti-Woodstock. We were witty and young
in a business that worshipped our youth, and just silly enough
to believe it always would.

The consummation-ending obsessed me, so the party
is something of a blur. In the small hours, I recall 6 or 7 guests
remaining, with one guy playing Dylan on his guitar.
I've seen love go by my door, never been this close before...
I caught her eye, and she smiled. Patience was not my
     strength.
*Crimson hair across your face, you could make me cry if you don't
     know.*

Alone at 3 a.m., we coupled, my 23-year-old body
like an unused bolt of lightning. We made love
in a weary hurry, a long shadow of inexperience
on experience making it clangy and a little jagged.
Desires were muddy and almost satisfied, but too many
choices and drug-distractions intruded.

On the last day, a mere 30,000 people left, arms aloft,
swaying to Hendrix. She described him burning his guitar.
Dawn came, she hitched home, roads clogged to the border.
I walked home in dusty, wrinkled white, Toronto in burnt
      orange
laid out before me. Our love affair was short, a 3-day festival
one summer long ago, where we would always be young.

Heretical

The risk – the danger – palpable.
The *are-you-enough* look she hands you
without even knowing that the curl of her lip
puts your entire manhood on a clothesline
to flap in the afternoon wind.

She is from Argentina. At least 30 years younger than I.
We are chatting from a distance, the only people
in a hotel breakfast room at 5 a.m., in a tiny European island
  town.

We will stop talking very soon, the time limit set by age.
At a certain point it becomes creepy. But she is from Argen-
  tina
and may not know that North American protocol.

Her nose tilts to point you to the perfect center of her top lip,
Her hair is a wild horse. Her beauty is striking,
and she may have no knowledge of it.

I have no fantasy that lasts more than two seconds now.
No expectation of such things that once crowded all
the others out. Youth is a blur.

On the long flights home, I try to describe
in words the tiny thrill of her existing
in a space where I also existed.

Eyes and hair, sulphuric dark on dark.
A lean blackness – coyote to the wolf –

plus that particular Argentinian touch
of old white Nazi Europe,
fleeing to a warmer unknown.

DAD

Dad

I wanted to be like you when I grew up,
until I grew up, which took forever,
when it finally occurred to me
that my lifelong idea-fear of you
was false.

You *were* afraid of things:
Flying, death, dying in particular ways,
ruin, your mother, your mother's
memory, fire, being ignorant,
me.

What power knowing that
would have bestowed upon me
as a young man, though
it would have destroyed
who I would become.

Maybe it's better I didn't know.
My children saw how afraid I was,
And look how that turned out.

Travelers

Homesickness is like asthma.
Some grow out of it. My strain
would strike as we pulled out
of the driveway, or got on the plane.

My older sister went to Europe for
her final year of high school, and we stood
at a fence, watching her walk, sobbing,
to the plane. And that person, 18-year-old
Paula, never returned. She still travels.

I didn't leave until I was 19, and my father
had to frighten me to make me go.
At the kitchen table, one idiotic spring evening,
he said, *You don't have to go to college.*
Monday we'll go to Imperial Oil and apprentice you
to a welder. And you'll do fine. He estimated what I'd make
the first year, but I wasn't listening. The word *welder*
startled me, stopped me cold, and I ran, never looking back
lest I be turned into a pillar of the community.

Topics

I write about age.
Or, more precisely, aging.
Skin-tag and thought-plain,
how all dreams end with some
authority figure saying Get up
and go to the bathroom before
you piss the bed.

I write about love you couldn't
see clearly. Fates crashed like parties.

I write about my father
as a younger man because
I'm not ready to write about him
as an old man or a dead man.
And that topic fits into
the love-fate-age triangle since
it took forever to see him, to see
his love for what it was, to see how
he sacrificed so his children would dare
what he did not.

Unerring

This is a story about instinct.
Something I possess but rarely trust.
One of the thousands of reasons I miss childhood is that
    freedom,
that ignorance.

I awoke in the night – bad dreams, no doubt –
a catch-all phrase for subconsciousness without history .
I was six years old. I came downstairs to find it empty.
But there was sound from the basement.

I assumed it was my father, and so I tried to open the door
very, very slowly, stopping at each pistol-shot creak to
    re-gauge
the subsequent silence and regulate my breathing.
Being scared was such delicious excitement.

Then the stairs down. I could see my father's head
above the back of the easy chair and I shiver-crawled
to a spot behind it. I could smell popcorn and tobacco.
I still can.

Why I didn't just call out to him
comes up in my mind now. He was always kind
and understanding of bad dreams. But I was too caught up
in playing secret-agent-superhero-stealth man.

My joyful invisibility ended when the telephone rang.
It was behind him on a side table. He got up and I correctly

assumed he'd go to his left, while I scurried around to the
front of the chair.
My instinct was sharp that night.

Curled into a ball, I realized my sneak-thief ingenuity
had run its reach. Discovery was inevitable now.
I didn't have much time. So again, I did
what I thought without thinking.

I stood up, facing him. He was talking on the phone
and I simply materialized in the room, like Houdini through
the wall.
It wasn't the first time I scared him.
It was the first time I realized I had.

Jesus CHRIST came out of him like a sneeze.
He hung up the phone and stared. Then he laughed,
came over and whisked me into his lap, and we
ate some popcorn and talked. He smelled fearless.

Images

The last ten years of his life were not upright ones,
full of steps and vigor. So images of him, walking, striding,
tall and bellied, carrying us all on his broad, birth-marked
    back,
are difficult to conjure.

At the kitchen table one winter night; Mother at the counter
as the door opened and his form and fortitude filled the
    room.
She turned to greet him and they kissed. I had a perfect side
    view
and the kiss broke with two lingering tongues visible for one
    searing second.

After dinner on autumn nights, we would say, "Passes, Dad?"
and he would get the football and my brother and I would
    run a few routes,
alternating between receiver and cornerback. Dad was the
    quarterback,
calling "Good catch!" or "Tough luck!"

One night at a big band concert in a ballroom, I saw he and
    mother dancing.
And they had obviously danced many times before. 'In The
    Mood' was playing
and they spin-waltzed around that room like they were part
    of a carousel,
with mother, a foot shorter, hanging on desperately to the
    giant she married.

Last image: On Sundays he would often spend the afternoon in his bedroom, on his bed, naked, reading a paperback.

If you came into the room, he would tent the novel over his genitals.

That's the one that stays with me.

The Call

So the call came.
So many now with the marketing *click*,
but not this one.

It was my sister,
and the pleat in my one-syllable name
left no doubt.
The doctor says he has three weeks.

Our father,
whose death we hated ourselves for imagining,
feared so long it got boring,
so long we forgot that it couldn't *not* happen,
had been given a final timeline.

They asked him to hold on
until I could get there. For a week,
my siblings, who all dwelt in a drive-able perimeter,
kept saying, *John's coming. Hold on for John.*
They filmed him saying hello to me, just in case.

I arrived – 2 flights, a car, and a border crossing –
at one a.m. and went straight to his hospital room.
He was sleeping. I stood there, 55 years of learning
how not to wake him up paying huge dividends,
and his eyes opened and he said, *What'd you bring me?*

He meant smokes. This 86 year old man,
barely able to move, dying of many cancers,
every breath a tussle, wanted a cigarette *so* badly.
It was only after he died that I realized it was
the last coherent thing he would ever say to me.

Dad & Poetry

One of the first poems I read out loud,
at his behest, was Housman's 'From Clee to Heaven'.
For some reason, childhood anger I suppose, I zipped
    through it,
finding neither meaning or gravity within its fine rhythmic
    lines.
He asked if I liked it. *It was okay*, I replied.
Because you read it like you didn't give a shit, he said,
flatly as a perfect fact can be stated.
The words burned, then as now.

Reading it today, knowing a little more,
I find it double-edged, in praise and grief.
The Golden jubilee of her majesty, Victoria,
and poets all must sing her high. But this poet
mourns the fallen, those She sent, now in their battle-crypts,
scattered across the globe. I'm sorry I read it
without knowing that, disappointing him.
And I can't tell him I get it now.

But something got me into poetry,
despite my natural inclination to reject
the things adults carped on about.
Dad never bought me a book of poems,
just showed me that it existed, this exalted thing,
in certain books. And after a certain age, I returned
to rediscover the man he called the greatest 'Roses-are-red,
violets-are-blue' poet ever.

In my teens, I saw a great English actor
read 'Bredon Hill on television one night, from memory,

and tears flowed from his eyes when he was finished.
The last line, 'I hear you. I will come', and the tears
sent me back to Housman. A poet friend who minces
neither praise or critique, says there are six or seven poems
in this group that are better than the entire canon
of many poets. We might disagree on which, but he's right.

In my second go-around, my father happened upon me
reading 'Oh see how thick the goldcup flowers' and offered
his interpretation of the girl's rejection, what exactly
she was turning down. I wonder now how much he thought
      I knew,
but he was blunt, as usual. '*So the boy is saying to her,*
Come lie down in this field with me, and maybe we'll
get into your pants', an expression I had not heard,
and never forgot. It floated up in every pursuit afterward.

And when, long past the chase myself, I read that Housman
was gay; spending his life in monkish scholarship to replace
      love
unspoken, I wanted to call Dad, triumphant – He *wasn't* try-
      ing
to get into her pants. He probably wanted a recipe for mince
      tarts
she was unwilling to share! One dreams of such intellectual
      vengeance.
Instead I sent the book , but Dad was past reading by then,
and soon after, past even discussing, so we never resumed the
      thread.
And now we won't. Housman will be mine alone.

Deathbed

His time-stained hands
gripped the railings of his bed,
like a prisoner not wishing to be
taken away. His mouth open to get
every last ounce of oxygen, each breath
a gasp going out through every muscle.

And then he saw me. And spoke,
but the sound came through his
hothouse lungs and bubbled up
into guttural gibberish. I tried to
imagine what it was, and I replied.
He let go of the railing. We both had to.

Father Time

On the phone, my sister says, "You know you're just like him,
don't you?", meaning our father, dead these fourteen months.

Later, I think, *no I'm not*. I no longer take any
of the numerous legal and illegal drugs
I'm addicted to. I can speak the name of my disease,
our disease, freely, and I remain more interested in
how it affects me than I am in who else obviously suffers
     from it
I love my profession and I'm not depressed most of the time.
I'm not in front of the TV watching *Judge Judy*, either.
I don't hate my mother and I'm not as stubborn
as a bloody concrete abutment.
And then I remember that I'm afraid of everything,
I dislike most people and avoid their company,
that a small lump anywhere means cancer everywhere,
that good luck only means bad luck is on the way.
I have a sharp tongue that hurts people, and a hair-trigger
temper, and I fear making a mistake so much
that I make hundreds of them. I married a good woman
and had children with her. I chose a profession that
induces worry. And deep down I hate my guts.

But I don't mention any of this
to my sister, who's a lot like him herself.

Olfactory

Sometimes I can smell my father.
Last night, for instance, sitting on my bed,
I smelled him. He's been dead three years
and three months. But he's with me.

The smell is a tobacco-terrycloth odor,
since those were his constants.
A generalized heated sweat in a dressing gown
and sixty-five years of Camel cigarettes.

Occasionally I see him in dreams,
but he never speaks. I always wait for him
to speak, but he just watches, as though his being
in my dream is a secret.

I know his voice, of course. It's with me.
Each time I smell him, I look around.
The window is usually open, which
is something ghosts wait for.

RAIN ISLAND

.

The Young in Vancouver

The young in Vancouver wear shorts on sunny days, because
their legs are beautiful. They walk and ride bicycles, sit behind
    glass
like artisanal bread in a thousand coffee shops, tattoos crowd-
    ing
out birthmarks, each one with a meaning and a story.

They sit in tiny oasis-parks with touchscreens, in ringing
    metabolic
shape, pleasing to the eye, liquid coolness, all color of hair,
    dark
against white skin, in a city so large it still has stores and
    people
who shop, with alcove lean-to's protecting the homeless in
    the rain.

The young in Vancouver smell of hope and potential and
    abandon,
appear to live well, bungee-muscles lean and whippy. They
    wear
sandals made of non-conflict rubber and hemp, shaped by
    sandal-craftsmen
who are paid a living wage in a country no one can spell.

They have a lot of sex, I assume, since there is no other
reason to be young in a perfect city by the sea. They sit
    down
only to eat and often get up in the middle of the meal
to dance, getting in their steps. Youth is their honesty.

Pouring out of concerts, mobbing eateries,
chatting in line, texting, touching, holding hands,
writing in moleskin journals, they live the never-ending days.
This morning I walked among them, unseen.

Five more Minutes

Dreamt I was lost
in Toronto,
so I must have
been very young.

I didn't like being lost,
but I stayed asleep
deep into the dream,
because I remembered
how much I enjoyed
being young.

Incognito

I don't know what I look like anymore.
At least I don't think I'm the guy
who should get those looks. *Who is this
creep and why is he staring at me?*
It's a male problem. The boy I was,
that boy's face, stares back at me
from a sixty year old trick mirror.
So I don't recognize the man
they think I look like, which is disorienting.
It always makes me look down,
and I see their shoes. Shoes don't judge.

Walking around a major city,
trying to get my steps in to lessen
my age-fat, standing in line
at a thousand coffeehouses,
women all around me and sometimes
I look and admittedly spend a moment
or two in that silly *she turns and our eyes
meet* fantasy that chases and charges me still
even though it's never happened.
Okay, maybe once. But I knew
what I looked like then.

Bad Bookstore

A bad bookstore Starbucks
on a coastal town Saturday evening,
and I write this with the quietly desperate
who can afford to sit on hardwood chairs
in windowed August.

Men who stare as though
the life they envisioned
is sitting a few feet away,
tauntingly content.

A morbidly obese woman of indefinite age –
which means *younger than I* – orange hair
and three muffins watches her computer,
having decided some hours ago that she would
go out on this Saturday night and experience life.

An older couple, out for a walk, have stopped
for a sit and two teas before trudging home to HBO.
They check their steps on iPhones.

Around us, books are set up for sale next to kitschy
cups and pillows with cute sayings on them: *Silent*
women rarely make history. If you slept here, you'd be
in bed by now. The kind of things you might buy for your
first apartment in your first town.

And we watch the light slowly extinguish itself
in roaring late-summer pink and orange, saying
nothing, other than the faded T-shirt manifestos
we thought described us well when we bought them.
I get up to leave our tiny asylum and no one
looks up from their warm screens.

New Worries

In the phone store,
the place where they grimace a little
when telling you their prices,
and you need to bring your passwords,

I looked around and realized
a gunman could just park his car out front,
stroll in and spray the place.

Would anyone look up from their screens
before dying? Would I throw myself down
behind the white composite-wood counter
for a few extra seconds of life?

No, I'd leap to shield my daughter,
taking the shots like a bodyguard.
Maybe. I hope I would.

Then I thought, rifle ammo
would go right through you
and kill her anyway.
But the protective instinct would trump that.

Luckily, the final price of a new phone
and plan made me forget how close
and random death is, forever.

Survival

Walking carefully
down from Russian Hill
in San Francisco,
steeper than a recurring nightmare,
I passed a homeless man
sitting on a concrete step,
shaving the sides of his head
with an old-fashioned
single edged razor,
using a bottle of water for moisture
and the blacked out window
of a dead store
as a mirror.

DNA

I sent the vial of spit
to the online DNA company.

My sister purchased the kit
as a Christmas gift,

because a second family member,
blood relative, male, would round out
her profile with risk assessment,
disease and age ranges likely for this strain
of white Dutch-Italian-German-Irish-English,
(the name neutral, the others at war).

Then I awaited the e-mail of discovery,
the 'land-ho!' chart of my ancestry-percentage.

Even though 2 months before the gift
arrived, I'd already been told
how I would die.

Rain Island

Whale Lake, I swam naked
in water that was cold and warm at the same time.
Stepped on rocks so ancient
they didn't know what feet were.

I was younger than my mother could remember.
We were alone, my friend had the only house
on this panoramic, evolutionary shore.

We rowed to Rain Island, ten backyards wide,
thick with virgin green. No legends here.
Only the spores had come.

Even scratches felt dignified, ritualistic.
We made moss angels, and then it rained
only where we were. The lake, two hundred feet away,
had no droplets.

I fished with a fly rod, catching two unwary trout.
Threw them back each with a story.
The darkness came so slowly
the world stopped aging.

I wanted to be naked, sketch glyphs
on a wall, paint my face, build fires,
dance to the sparks, invent
a language I could sing.

Books by John Wing

Poetry

A Cup Of Nevermind (Mosaic Press) 1998
...And The Fear Makes Us Special (Mosaic Press) 2000
Ventriloquism For Dummies (Black Moss Press) 2002
None Of This Is Probably True (Mosaic Press) 2003
Excuses (Mosaic Press) 2005
The Winter Palace (Mosaic Press) 2007
When The Red Light Goes On, Get Off (Black Moss Press) 2008
So Recently Ancient (Mosaic Press) 2010
Almost Somewhere Else (Mosaic Press) 2012
Why-Shaped Scars (Black Moss Press) 2014
I'll Be There Soon (Black Moss Press) 2016
The Last Coherent Thing (Mosaic Press) 2021

Fiction

A Car To Die For (Mosaic Press) 2021

Acknowledgements

A few years ago, my first real poetry teacher, other than my father, John Ditsky, died suddenly. He had never warmed to e-mail, so our correspondence had all but stopped for a few years. Then it started up again. I was writing my second return letter when he died. When I began writing the poems included in this book, my longtime first reader and childhood acquaintance of my father, Don Coles, was still alive to offer his wonderful guidance and advice. But now he too is gone. My father died in 2017, a month short of his 87th birthday. The three of them are mourned and missed by me, as well as others.

The poems here have not been published before. I no longer have the excuse of being on the road so much that I never send them to literary magazines, since the 2020-21 pandemic has kept me at home for 13 months. But I still don't. So here they are in all their glory, so to speak. Thanks to Howard and Jeannette and everyone at Mosaic Press, my family, Lisa Novick-Warner, and especially to my wife, who still lives with me after 33 years.

John Wing Jr.

Born in Sarnia, Ontario, John started as a standup comedian in Toronto in 1980, moving on to Los Angeles in 1988. He has over 300 television appearances to his credit, including six *Tonight Shows*, with both Johnny Carson and Jay Leno. A regular performer at comedy festivals, John has headlined at the Montreal *Just For Laughs Festival* as well as the Winnipeg, Vancouver, Edmonton, Niagara Falls, Toronto, and Halifax Comedy Festivals, racking up over fifty in his long career. In 2013, John was a semi-finalist on *America's Got Talent*, performing three times at *Radio City Music Hall*. For many years, he's performed his comedy on cruise ships around the world, *including Holland America, Royal Caribbean, Norwegian, Carnival*, and *Celebrity Cruise Lines*.

He published his first book of poems in 1998. *The Last Coherent Thing* is his tenth collection. *A Car To Die For* is his first novel. Since April of 2020, John has written and performed the podcast *The Bad Piano Player*, now with more than fifty episodes available for download. Married for 32 years to Dawn Greene, with two grown daughters, John lives in Los Angeles, California.